The Cheshire Cat and Other Eye-Popping Experiments on How We See the World

THE EXPLORATORIUM SCIENCE SNACKBOOK SERIES

The Cheshire Cat and Other Eye-Popping
Experiments on How We See the World

The Magic Wand and Other Bright
Experiments on Light and Color

And coming in spring of 1996 . . .

The Cool Hot Rod and Other Electrifying
Experiments on Energy and Matter

The Spinning Blackboard and Other Dynamic
Experiments on Force and Motion

The Cheshire Cat
and Other Eye-Popping
Experiments on
How We See the World

THE EXPLORATORIUM SCIENCE
SNACKBOOK SERIES

PAUL DOHERTY, DON RATHJEN
and the Exploratorium Teacher Institute

JOHN WILEY & SONS, INC.
New York · Chichester · Brisbane · Toronto · Singapore

To the many teachers of the Exploratorium Teacher Institute

who enthusiastically developed and tested the materials

in this book.

Development and Testing   Teachers of the Exploratorium Teacher Institute
Photography   Esther Kutnick, Susan Schwartzenberg, Amy Snyder
Illustrations   Larry Antila, Jad King, Arthur Koch, Luisa Kolla, Peter Olguin

This text is printed on acid-free paper.

Library of Congress Cataloging-in-Publication Data:

Doherty, Paul.
     The Cheshire cat and other eye-popping experiments on how we see the world / Paul Doherty, Don Rathjen, and the Exploratorium Teacher Institute.
          p.   cm. — (The Exploratorium science snackbook series)
     Includes index.
     ISBN 0-471-11516-9
     1. Visual perception—Experiments—Juvenile literature.   [1. Visual perception—Experiments.   2. Experiments.]   I. Rathjen, Don.   II. Exploratorium Teacher Institute (San Francisco, Calif.)   III. Title.   IV. Series.
QP441.D64   1995
152.14'078—dc20   94-47034

Printed in the United States of America

10 9 8 7 6 5 4 3 2 1

Contents

Welcome to the Exploratorium Science Snackbook Series

This book is full of Snacks . . .

. . . but they're not the kind you eat. They're the kind you can learn from and have fun with.

Exploratorium Science Snacks are miniature versions of some of the most popular exhibits at the Exploratorium, San Francisco's famed museum of science, art, and human perception.

What's different about the Exploratorium?

For lack of a better description, the Exploratorium calls itself a "museum." But the half-million visitors who come through the doors each year don't find hushed corridors, watchful guards, or "do not touch" signs. Instead, they walk into a cavernous space filled with whirring, buzzing, spinning things, where people of all ages are smiling and laughing and calling to each other to "Come see this!" and "Hey, look at that!"

At the Exploratorium, you can touch a tornado, look inside your eye, or leave your shadow on a wall. You can pull a giant bubble over your head, sing your way through a maze, or tour a pitch-dark labyrinth using only your sense of touch. When you're done, you might find that you understand a little more about weather, or your senses, or the nature of a bubble film, than you've ever understood before.

So what's a Science Snack?

Since the museum opened in 1969, teachers from the San Francisco Bay Area have brought their classes on field trips to the Exploratorium. When we began putting this book together, we decided to do just the opposite: We wanted to take the exhibits to the kids.

For three years, nearly one hundred teachers worked with staff members to create scaled-down versions of Exploratorium exhibits. The results were dozens of exciting "Snacks"— miniature science exhibits that teachers could make using common, inexpensive, easily available materials. By using Snacks in their classrooms, teachers can climb out of their textbooks and join their students in discovering science for themselves.

What's in a Snack?

The Snacks in this book are divided into easy-to-follow sections that include instructions, advice, and helpful hints.

Each Snack begins with a drawing of the original, full-sized exhibit on the museum floor and a photograph of the scaled-down version that you can make yourself. A short paragraph introduces the exhibit. There's a list of the materials needed and suggestions on how to find them. Other sections give assembly instructions, contain descriptions of how to use the completed exhibits, and explain the science behind them. Most of the Snacks can be completed by one person. If a partner or adult help is needed, this is indicated. A section called "etc." offers interesting bits of additional scientific and historic information.

What can you do with a Snack?

The original collection of 107 Science Snacks was published in a single volume called *The Exploratorium Science Snackbook*. Although the book was written for local high school science teachers, it wasn't long before we began to realize that Snacks were really getting around. Within a week of publication, for instance, we received a message from a teacher in the Australian outback who needed help finding materials.

We heard from elementary school teachers and university professors. Art teachers were using Snacks, as were shop teachers and math teachers. Sixth-graders at one school were building their own miniature science museum. At another school, an ESL (English as a Second Language) teacher found that building Snacks helped her students interact more: Those who understood science best were helping those more adept at building things, and all were getting better at communicating with each other.

And it wasn't just teachers who found Snacks useful: Children were bringing Snacks home to their families. Scouts were using Snacks to help get science badges; Snacks were making appearances at science fairs, birthday parties, and impromptu "magic" shows.

Try it for yourself!

Until now, Science Snacks were available only to teachers. The books in this series now make Science Snacks available to anyone interested in learning about science, or helping others learn about science. Try it for yourself! You might be delighted to find how well hands-on discovery works.

Acknowledgments

The production of the original *Exploratorium Science Snackbook*,
upon which this book is based, was made possible
by a grant from

The Telesis Foundation

The Snackbook was developed by the Teacher Institute, a part
of the Exploratorium Regional Science Resource Center, which
is funded in part by

California Department of Education
National Science Foundation
Walter S. Johnson Foundation

What This Book Is About

How do you see the world around you? You open your eyes and there it is: your room, your desk, the pictures on the walls, the trees outside your window.

When you take a look at the world, here's what's happening: Light is bouncing off the pictures, the trees, and all the things out there in the world. Some of that light gets into your eye. This light shines through the cornea, the tough clear covering over the front of your eye, and then through the pupil, the dark hole in the center of your iris, the colored part of your eye. Your eye's lens focuses this light to make an image on your retina, a thin layer of light-sensitive cells that lines the back of your eyeball. The light-sensitive cells of the retina signal the brain, and the brain creates a mental image. Finally, you see the world out there.

People have compared the eye to a camera—for good reason. Both your eye and a camera have adjustable openings that let in light: the pupil of your eye and the aperture of a camera. Both focus the light to make an image on a light-sensitive screen: the retina of your eye and the film of a camera.

But unlike a camera, your eye doesn't just passively record the image it receives. Working together, your eyes and brain decide what to see and how to see it. They fill in gaps in your visual field, taking limited information and creating a complete picture. They interpret the limited and distorted images that they receive and try to make sense of the world out there, often using past experience as a guide. They constantly filter out and ignore extraneous information.

You don't believe me? Then close one eye and take a look at the tip of your nose. You can see it clearly if you think about it. It's always in your view. Open both eyes and you can still see it, a shadowy protuberance in the center of your visual field. If you think about the tip of your nose, you can see it—but most of the time, you don't notice it (even though it's as plain as the nose on your face).

The experiments in this book will show you some other sights that you usually don't notice. Some experiments, such as Blind Spot, Pupil, and Afterimage, will help you understand more about how your eye works—its abilities and limitations. Others, like Vanna and Far Out Corners, show how prior experience often influences perception: how what you "see" may not be what you "get." Still others, like Persistence of Vision and Jacques Cousteau in Seashells, demonstrate that your eyes and brain can take very limited information and create a complete picture of the world. Finally, some show how your eyes and brain can make mistakes in their interpretation of the world— mistakes that create optical illusions, deceptive pictures that fool your eyes.

Taken together, these experiments let you explore visual perception, a fascinating interdisciplinary topic, where biology and psychology overlap. Have fun!

Afterimage

A flash of light prints a lingering image in your eye.

▶ After looking at something bright—such as a lamp or a camera's flash—you may continue to see an image of that object when you look away. This lingering visual impression is called an **afterimage**.

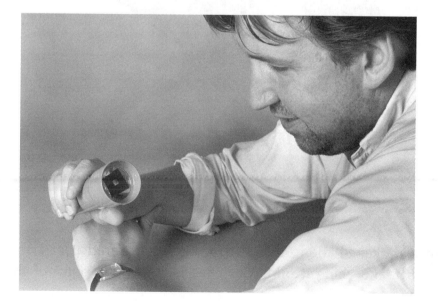

Materials ► A flashlight.

► White paper.

► Opaque black tape (such as electrical tape).

Assembly
(15 minutes or less)

Tape a piece of white paper over a flashlight lens. Cover most of this paper with strips of opaque tape. In the center of the lens, leave an area uncovered, so that the light can shine through the paper. This area should be a square, a triangle, or some other simple, recognizable shape.

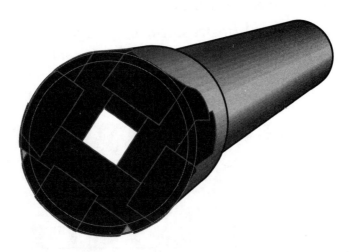

To Do and Notice
(15 minutes or more)

In a darkened room, turn on the flashlight, hold it at arm's length, and shine it into your eyes. Stare at one point of the brightly lit shape for about 30 seconds. Then stare at a blank wall and blink a few times. Notice the shape and color of the image you see.

Try again—first focusing on the palm of your hand, and then focusing on a wall some distance from you. Compare the size of the image you see in your hand to the image you see on the wall.

Close your left eye and stare at the bright image with your right eye. Then close your right eye and look at the white wall with your left eye. You will not see an afterimage.

What's Going On?

You see because light enters your eyes and produces chemical changes in the *retina*, the light-sensitive lining at the back of your eyes. Prolonged stimulation by a bright image (here, the light source) desensitizes part of the retina. When you look at the white wall, light reflecting from the wall shines onto your retina. The area of the retina that was desensitized by the bright image does not respond as well to this new light input as the rest of the retina. This area appears as a *negative afterimage,* a dark area that matches the original shape. The afterimage may remain for 30 seconds or longer.

The apparent size of the afterimage depends not only on the size of the image on your retina, but also on how far away you perceive the image to be. When you look at your hand, you see the negative afterimage on your hand. Because your hand is near you, you see the image as relatively small—no bigger than your hand. When you look at a distant wall, you see the negative afterimage on the wall. But it is not the same size as the afterimage you saw on your hand. You see the afterimage on the wall as much bigger—large enough to cover a considerable area of the wall. The afterimage is not actually on either surface, but on your retina. The actual afterimage does not change size; only your interpretation of its size changes.

This helps explain a common illusion that you may have noticed. The full moon often appears larger when it is on the horizon than when it is overhead. The disk of the moon is the exact same size in both cases, and its image on your retina is also the same size. So why does the moon look bigger in one position than in the other? One explanation suggests that you perceive the horizon as farther away than the sky overhead. This perception might lead you to see the moon as a large disk when it is near the horizon (just as you saw the afterimage as larger when you thought it was on the distant wall), and as a smaller disk when it is overhead (just like the smaller afterimage in the palm of your hand).

Negative afterimages do not transfer from one eye to the other. This indicates that they are produced on the retina, and not in the visual cortex of the brain where the signals would have been fused together.

○ ○ ○ ○ ○ ○   **etc.**   ○ ○ ○ ○ ○ ○

For up to 30 minutes after you walk into a dark room, your eyes are adapting. At the end of this time, your eyes may be up to 10,000 times more sensitive to light than they were when you entered the room. We call this improved ability to see *night vision.* It is caused by the chemical *rhodopsin,* in the rods of your retina. Rhodopsin, popularly called *visual purple,* is a light-sensitive chemical composed of vitamin A and the protein *opsin.*

You can use the increased presence of rhodopsin to take "afterimage photographs" of the world. Here's how.

Cover your eyes to allow them to adapt to the dark. Be careful that you do not press on your eyeballs. It will take at least 10 minutes to store up enough visual purple to take a "snapshot." When enough time has elapsed, uncover your eyes. Open your eyes and look at a well-lit scene for half a second (just long enough to focus on the scene), then close and cover your eyes again. You should see a detailed picture of the scene in purple and black. After a while, the image will reverse to black and purple. You may take several "snapshots" after each 10-minute adaptation period.

For a more complete desciption of this experiment, see Paul Hewitt's *Conceptual Physics Lab Manual* (HarperCollins College Publishers, New York, 1993).

Anti-Gravity Mirror

It's all done with mirrors!

▶ A reflection of your right side can appear to be your left side. With this Snack, you can appear to perform many gravity-defying stunts.

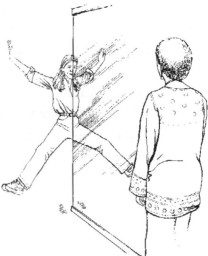

Materials ▸ A large, flat, plastic mirror, 2 × 3 feet (60 × 90 cm) or larger. (It is important to get a good, flat mirror, since distortions will ruin the effect.) Plastic mirrors are expensive, but glass mirrors can be dangerous. Look in your local yellow pages for a nearby plastics store.

▸ A length of 2 × 4 inch wood and a router tool, or ring stands and clamps, to make a stand to hold the mirror upright.

▸ Optional: A sturdy table on which you can stand.

▸ A partner. Adult help.

Assembly
(with stand: 15 minutes or less; without: 5 minutes or less)

You can make a stand for the mirror from a length of 2 × 4 inch wood. Use a router to cut a groove that is just wide enough to slip the mirror into. To help stabilize the mirror, you can nail some scrap wood to the ends of the board. You can also hold the mirror in a vertical position using ring stands and clamps, or just with your hands (an assistant might be of help here).

To Do and Notice
(15 minutes or more)

Stand the mirror on the floor or on a sturdy table. Put one leg on each side of the mirror. Shift your weight to the foot behind the

mirror. Lift your other leg and move it repeatedly toward and away from the mirror. To an observer, you'll appear to be flying. If you use this Snack as a demonstration, you can make the effect more dramatic by covering the mirror with a cloth, climbing onto the table, straddling the mirror, and then dropping the cloth as you "take off."

What's Going On?

A person standing with the edge of a large mirror bisecting his or her body will appear whole to a person who's watching. To the observer, the mirror image of the left half of a person looks exactly like the real right half. Or if the person is standing on the opposite end of the mirror, the right half looks like the real left half. The person looks whole because the human body is symmetrical. The observer's brain is tricked into believing that an image of your right side is really your left side. So just straddle the mirror, raise one leg, and you'll fly!

○ ○ ○ ○ ○ ○ **etc.** ○ ○ ○ ○ ○ ○

Try this out in department stores that have full-length mirrors available. If your school has a dance room with a mirrored wall and a doorway cut into it, you may be able to use it. With these full mirrors, stand at the edge of the doorway so that just half of your body is being reflected. This will be an even more convincing flight.

The cars that floated across the desert in the movie *Star Wars* each had a full-length mirror attached along their lower edge, hiding the wheels. A camera pointed at a car saw a view of reflected sand and shadow in the mirror. That is how the cars appeared to float above the sand.

Benham's Disk

A rotating black-and-white disk produces the illusion of color.

▶ When you rotate this black-and-white pattern at the right speed, the pattern appears to contain colored rings. You see color because the different color receptors in your eyes respond at different rates.

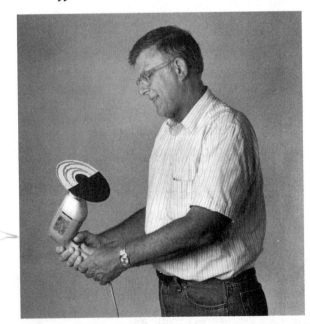

Materials ▸ Posterboard or cardboard.

▸ Glue stick or other suitable adhesive.

▸ Pattern disk (provided here).

▸ Access to a copy machine.

▸ A black marking pen.

▸ A rotator. You can use a turntable, variable speed electric drill, hand drill, portable electric mixer, or electric screw driver. Attach the disk with adhesive Velcro™, or if a drill with a chuck is used, a bolt can be used as a shaft, with two nuts to hold the disk. You can also reduce the size of the disk on a copy machine, then mount it on the flat upper surface of a suitable toy top, or you can devise your own spinner for the disk. Try spinning the mounted disk on a pencil point, or on a pushpin stuck into a pencil eraser.

▸ Adult help.

Assembly
(15 minutes or less)

Copy the pattern disk in the drawing on the next page and mount it on a cardboard backing with the adhesive. If your copier does not make good solid blacks, fill in the black areas with a black marking pen. You can reduce or enlarge the pattern disk if you like.

Attach the mounted disk to a rotator. (See the Materials section for rotator and mounting suggestions.)

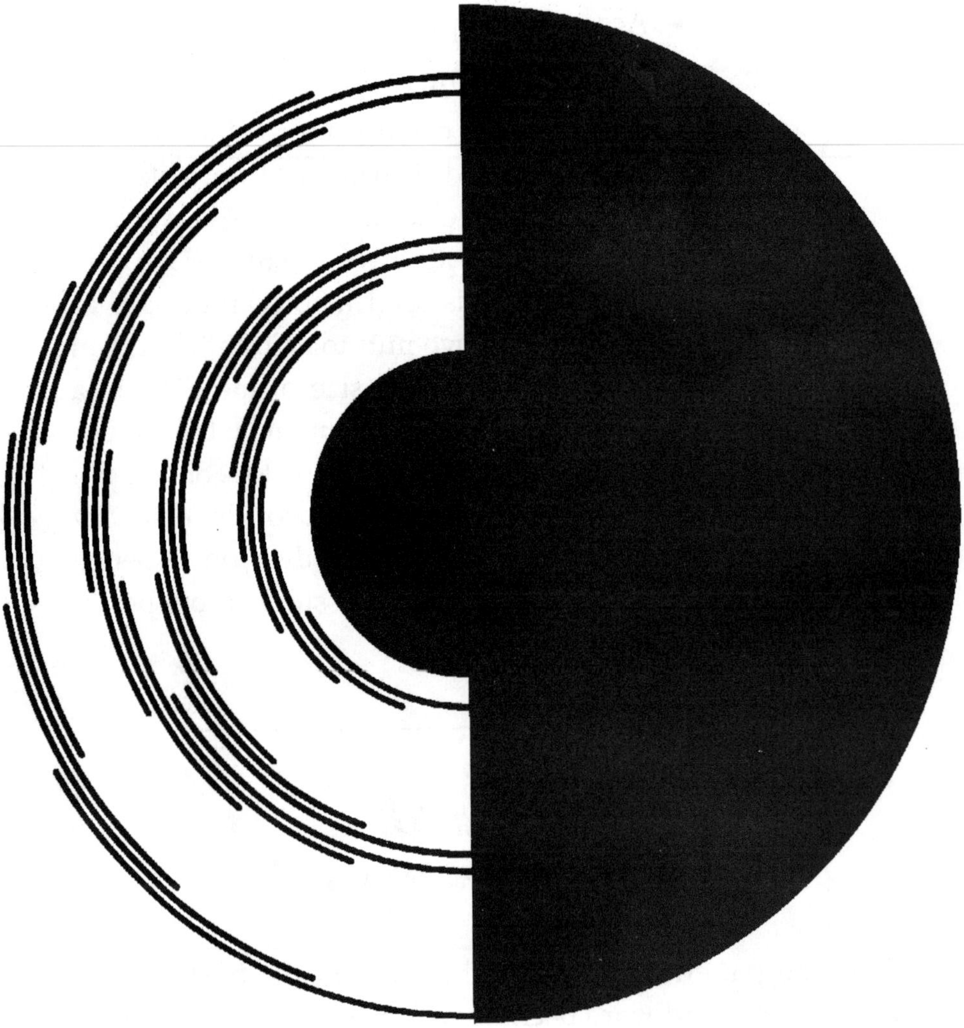

To Do and Notice
(15 minutes or more)

Spin the disk under bright incandescent light or sunlight. (Fluorescent light will work, but there is a strobing effect that gives the disk a pulsating appearance and makes it harder to look at.)

Notice the colored bands that appear on the disk. Look at the order the colors are in. What color do you see at the center? What about the next few bands?

Reverse the direction of rotation and compare the order of colors again, from the center of the disk to the rim.

Try varying the speed of rotation and the size of the pattern, and compare the results with your initial observations.

What's Going On?

Different people see different intensities of colors on this spinning disk. Just why people see color here is not fully understood, but the illusion involves color vision cells in your eyes called *cones*.

There are three types of cones. One is most sensitive to red light, one to green light, and one to blue light. Each type of cone has a different *latency* time, the time it takes to respond to a color, and a different *persistence of response* time, the time it keeps responding after the stimulus has been removed. Blue cones, for example, are the slowest to respond (have the longest latency time), and keep responding the longest (have the longest persistence time).

When you gaze at one place on the spinning disk, you are looking at alternating flashes of black and white. When a white flash goes by, all three types of cones respond. But your eyes and brain see the color white only when all three types of cones are responding equally. The fact that some types of cones respond more quickly than others—and that some types of cones keep responding longer than others—leads to an imbalance that partly explains why you see colors.

The colors vary across the disk because at different radial positions on the disk the black arcs have different lengths, so that the flashing rate they produce on the retina is also different.

The explanation of the colors produced by Benham's disk is more complicated than the simple explanation outlined above. For example, the short black arcs that are on all Benham's disks must also be thin, or no colors will appear.

○ ○ ○ ○ ○ ○   **etc.**   ○ ○ ○ ○ ○ ○

Benham's disk was invented by a nineteenth-century toymaker who noticed colors in a black-and-white pattern he had mounted on a top. Toy spinning tops with Benham's disks are still available in the Exploratorium Store and in toy stores.

The three different color sensors in a color television camera also have different latency and persistence times. When a color television camera sweeps across a bright white light in its field of view, it often produces a colored streak across the television screen.

When your eye scans a black-and-white pattern containing fine detail, you will sometimes see subtle colors. For more information, see the book *Seeing the Light,* by David Falk, Dieter Brill, and David Stork (Harper & Row, 1986).

Bird in the Cage

Stare at a color and see it change.

▶ You see color when receptor cells (called **cones**) on your eye's retina are stimulated by light. There are three types of cones, each sensitive to a particular color range. If one or more of the three types of cones becomes fatigued to the point where it responds less strongly than it normally would, the color you perceive from a given object will change.

Materials
▸ 4 white posterboards or pieces of paper.

▸ Bright red, green, and blue construction or contact paper.

▸ Small piece of black construction or contact paper, or black marking pen.

▸ Scissors.

▸ Glue or glue stick (if you are using construction paper).

▸ Adult help.

Assembly
(30 minutes or less)

Cut the same simple shape, such a bird or a fish, from each of the three colored papers. Glue each shape on its own white board. Leave one white board blank. Cut a small black eye for each bird or fish or draw one in with the marking pen. If you choose a bird as the shape, draw the outline of a birdcage on the blank board; if you choose a fish, draw a fishbowl, etc. (Be creative!)

To Do and Notice
(15 minutes or more)

Place the boards in a well-lit area. (Bright lighting is a significant factor in making this Snack work well.)

Stare at the eye of the red bird for 15 to 20 seconds and then quickly stare at the birdcage. You should see a bluish-green (cyan) bird in the cage. Now repeat the process, staring at the green bird. You should see a reddish-blue (magenta) bird in the cage. Finally, stare at the blue bird. You should see a yellow bird in the cage. (If you used a fish, try the same procedure with the fish and the bowl.)

What's Going On?

The ghostly fishes and birds that you see here are called *after-images.* An afterimage is an image that stays with you even after you have stopped looking at the object.

The back of your eye is lined with light-sensitive cells called *rods* and *cones.* Cones are sensitive to colored light, and each of the three types of cones is sensitive to a particular range of color.

When you stare at the red bird, the image falls on one region of your retina. The red-sensitive cells in that region start to grow tired and stop responding strongly to red light. The white board reflects red, blue, and green light to your eyes (since white light is made up of all these colors). When you suddenly shift your gaze to the blank white board, the fatigued red-sensitive cells don't respond to the reflected red light, but the blue-sensitive and green-sensitive cones respond strongly to the reflected blue and green light. As a result, where the red-sensitive cells don't respond you see a bluish-green bird. This bluish-green color is called *cyan.*

When you stare at the green bird, your green-sensitive cones become fatigued. Then, when you look at the white board, your eyes respond only to the reflected red and blue light, and you see a red-blue, or *magenta,* bird. Similarly, when you stare at a blue object, the blue-sensitive cones become fatigued, and the reflected red and green light combine to form yellow.

○ ○ ○ ○ ○ ○   **etc.**   ○ ○ ○ ○ ○ ○

You can design other objects with different colored paper and predict the results. Try a blue banana! For smaller versions, you can use brightly colored stickers (from stationery, card, or gift stores) on index cards.

One classic variation of this experiment uses an afterimage to make the American flag. Draw a flag, but substitute alternating green and black stripes for the familiar red and white stripes, and black stars on a yellow field for the white stars on a blue field. For simplicity, you can idealize the flag with a few thick stripes and a few large stars. When you stare at the flag and then stare at a blank white background, the flag's afterimage will appear in the correct colors.

You may also want to experiment with changing the distance between your eyes and the completely white board while you are observing the afterimage. Notice that the perceived size of the image changes, even though the size of the fatigued region on your retina remains the same. The perceived size of an image depends on both the size of the image on your retina and the perceived distance to the object. (For more information on afterimages, see page 3.)

Blind Spot

To see, or not to see.

▶ The eye's retina receives and reacts to incoming light and sends signals to the brain, allowing you to see. There is, however, a part of the retina that doesn't give you visual information. This is your eye's blind spot.

Materials ▸ One 3 × 5 inch (8 × 13 cm) card or other stiff paper.

▸ A meterstick.

Assembly
(5 minutes or less)

Mark a dot and a cross on a card as shown.

To Do and Notice
(5 minutes or more)

Hold the card at eye level about an arm's length away. Make sure that the cross is on the right.

Close your right eye and look directly at the cross with your left eye. Notice that you can also see the dot. Focus on the cross but be aware of the dot as you slowly bring the card toward your face. The dot will disappear, and then reappear, as you bring the card toward your face.

Now close your left eye and look directly at the dot with your right eye. This time the cross will disappear and reappear as you bring the card slowly toward your face.

Try the activity again, this time rotating the card so that the dot and cross are not directly across from each other. Are the results the same?

What's Going On?

The optic nerve carries messages from your eye to your brain. This bundle of nerve fibers passes through one spot on the light-sensitive lining, or *retina,* of your eye. In this spot, your eye's retina has no light receptors. When you hold the card so that the light from the dot falls on this spot, you cannot see the dot.

As a variation on this blind spot activity, draw a straight line across the card, from one edge to the other, through the center of the cross and the dot. Notice that when the dot disappears, the line appears to be continuous, without a gap where the dot used to be. Your brain automatically "fills in" the blind spot with a simple extrapolation of the image surrounding the blind spot. This is why you do not notice the blind spot in your day-to-day observations of the world.

○ ○ ○ ○ ○ ○   **etc.**   ○ ○ ○ ○ ○ ○

Using a simple model for the eye, you can find the approximate size of the blind spot on the retina.

Mark a cross on the left edge of a 3 × 5 inch (8 × 13 cm) card. Hold the card 9.75 inches (25 cm) from your eye. (You will need to measure this distance; your distance from the card is important in determining the size of your blind spot.)

Close your left eye and look directly at the cross with your right eye. Move a pen on the card until the point of the pen disappears in your blind spot. Mark the places where the penpoint disappears. Use the pen to trace the shape and size of your blind spot on the card. Measure the diameter of the blind spot on the card.

In our simple model, we are assuming that the eye behaves like a pinhole camera, with the pupil as the pinhole. In such a model, the pupil is 0.78 inches (2 cm) from the retina. Light travels in a straight line through the pupil to the retina. Similar triangles can then be used to calculate the size of the blind spot on your retina. The simple equation for this calculation is $s/2 = d/D$, where s is the diameter of the blind spot on your retina, d is the size of the blind spot on the card, and D is the distance from your eye to the card (in this case, 9.75 inches [25 cm]).

$$s/2 = d/D$$

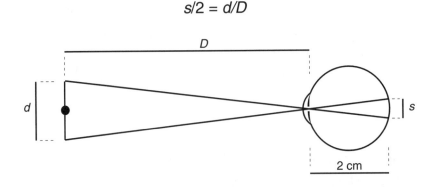

Bronx Cheer Bulb

Some lightbulbs may appear to wiggle and flash when you give them the raspberry, but the only thing wiggling is you.

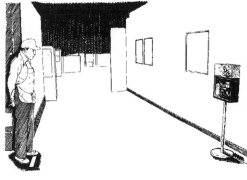

▶ *Some light sources flash on and off many times a second. When you give them the "Bronx cheer," you can see the hidden flickering of light sources.*

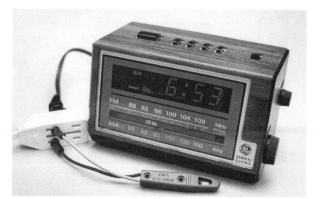

Materials ▶ A digital radio or clock radio that uses light-emitting diodes (LEDs). These have red numbers.

or

▶ A circuit tester with an LED on it.

or

▶ A neon glow lamp available from your local hardware store, such as a GE Guide lamp, and an extension cord. (Any night-light labeled "¼ watt" has a neon glow lamp in it).

Assembly
(5 minutes or less)

No assembly is required for the digital radio, circuit tester, or neon glow lamp; just plug them in and observe them from a few feet away.

A simple source for a neon glow lamp is a button-type night-light. These are small orange night-lights advertised as ¼ watt bulbs. They do not have a regular replaceable small lightbulb. Plug the night-light into the wall or into an extension cord that is plugged in.

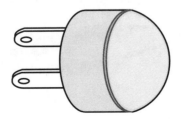

To Do and Notice
(5 minutes or more)

Observe the light source from 3 to 10 feet (90 to 300 cm) away and give it the "Bronx cheer." (A Bronx cheer, also known as a "raspberry," is a rude noise made by blowing air through your lips in a way that makes them vibrate.) Notice that the light seems to wiggle back and forth and flicker. Try shaking your head rapidly and notice whether the light still flickers. See if you can find other body motions that make the light flicker. Try the Bronx cheer on other light sources, such as incandescent light-bulbs. Notice whether the light flickers.

What's Going On?

No part of the LEDs or the neon glow tube move when you give the Bronx cheer. Instead, your whole body is vibrating, including your eyes. You can feel this vibration by putting your hand on your head as you blow. The LEDs flash on and off sixty times a second (a neon glow tube glows on and off 120 times a second). This flashing is so fast that your eyes normally can't separate the "blinks." But when your body is vibrating, your eyes are in a different position each time the bulb flashes. As the image of the bulb traces a path across your eyes, it looks like the bulb is moving and flickering.

An incandescent bulb won't flicker when you give the Bronx cheer, because the bulb doesn't flash on and off. Incandescent bulbs give a steady glow.

○ ○ ○ ○ ○ ○   **etc.**   ○ ○ ○ ○ ○ ○

Plug a commercial neon night-light into an extension cord. Tape it firmly in place. Twirl the light around in a circle. (Be careful not to let it hit anything.) Notice that you can see the light flashing. Since the light is moving, it's in a new position each time it flashes. The light traces a path across your eye, and its flashes become spread out and visible.

Find an oscilloscope and set it up so that the beam goes straight across the middle of the screen in about 1/100th of a second. Ask a couple of friends to stand back a few yards from the scope. Tell them that the oscilloscope is an eating detector. Have your friends watch the scope at the same time. Have one of them eat a peanut and the other one not eat. The person eating the peanut will see the beam jump up and down. Eating causes vibrations of your skull, including vibrations of your eyes. If your eyes are moving, the dot of light scanning across the oscilloscope shines on different parts of your eyes and appears to jump around.

Cardboard Tube Syllabus

Your brain combines information from your eyes in surprising ways.

▶ You have two eyes, yet you see only one image of your environment. If your eyes receive conflicting information, what does your brain do? Do receptors in the eye act independently, or do they influence each other? By looking through some simple tubes made from rolled-up pieces of paper, you can explore how your two eyes influence each other.

Materials ▸ A well-lit white screen, white wall, or white sheet of paper.

▸ Several sheets of white paper, such as typing paper or photocopy paper.

▸ Transparent tape.

Assembly
(5 minutes or less)

Roll three of the sheets of paper into paper tubes that are 11 inches (28 cm) long and about ½ inch (1.3 cm) in diameter. Use tape to keep the tubes from unrolling. Squash one of the tubes so that its cross-section is a very flat oval.

Cut one piece of paper into a strip that is about 2½ inches (6.4 cm) wide and 11 inches (28 cm) long. Roll this strip into a tube that is about ½ inch (1.3 cm) in diameter and 11 inches (28 cm) long.

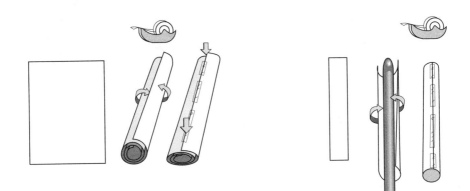

Hole in Your Hand

To Do and Notice
(5 minutes or more)

Take one of the tubes that you made from a full sheet of paper in your right hand. Hold it up to your right eye and look through the tube, keeping both eyes open.

Now put your left hand, fingers up, palm toward your face, up against the left side of the tube, about two-thirds of the way down. Notice that you see a hole in your hand.

What's Going On?

One eye sees a hole, the other sees a hand. Your eyes and brain add the two images together, creating a hand with a hole in it!

Overlapping Spots
To Do and Notice
(5 minutes or more)

Take two round tubes that you made from full sheets of paper. Put the tubes up to your eyes and look through them at the white screen, wall, or sheet of paper. First close one eye, and then open it and close the other. Does the brightness of the spot appear the same for each eye?

Move the tubes to overlap the two spots. Notice that there is a brighter area where the two spots overlap.

Overlap the spots completely. Does the combined spot look brighter than either spot alone? Find out by closing one eye.

What's Going On?

When you partly overlap the two spots, your open eye and brain conclude that the sum of the two spots of light should be brighter than one spot alone. If the spots overlap completely, the brain seems to ignore one of them.

Circles or Ovals
To Do and Notice
(5 minutes or more)

Hold one of the round tubes up to one eye and the tube that you flattened up to the other eye. Look through the tubes at the white screen, wall, or paper. Overlap the spots. Do you see the circle or the oval? Switch the tubes and repeat. If you saw only the circle before, you may see the oval now.

What's Going On?

Your eyes and brain have trouble merging the different shapes. Most people have a dominant eye. The brain will choose to see the image that is coming from the dominant eye. Some people do not have a dominant eye, and therefore see the two shapes overlapped. The best baseball hitters do not have a dominant eye.

Lateral Inhibition

To Do and Notice
(5 minutes or more)

With both eyes open, look at the white screen, wall, or paper through one of the tubes you made from a full sheet of paper. Notice that the spot of light that you see through the tube appears brighter than the wall of the tube.

Do the same thing using the tube that you made from a strip of paper. Notice that the spot appears darker than the wall of the tube.

What's Going On?

When light receptors in your eyes receive light, they send a signal to your brain. A receptor receiving light also sends signals to neighboring receptors, telling them to turn down their own sensitivity to light. When you look at the white wall without a tube, you see a uniform field of brightness because all the receptors are equally inhibited. When you look through the tube that you made from a full sheet of paper, the spot of light is surrounded by the dark ring of the tube. The spot appears brighter because the receptors in the center of your retina are not inhibited by signals from the surrounding dark ring.

In contrast, light shines through the walls of the tube that you made from a strip of paper. When you look through this thin-walled tube, the spot appears darker because light comes through the wall of the tube, causing the receptors at the center of your retina to be inhibited. This is known as *lateral inhibition.*

○ ○ ○ ○ ○ ○   **etc.**   ○ ○ ○ ○ ○ ○

You can use paper towel tubes for all but the last of these experiments.

Cheshire Cat

Make a friend disappear, leaving only a smile behind.

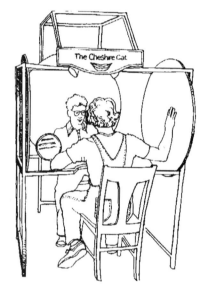

▶ Under most circumstances, both of your eyes receive fairly similar views of the of the world around you. You fuse these views into a single three-dimensional picture. This Snack lets you explore what happens when your eyes receive different images.

Materials ► A handheld mirror, approximately 4 to 6
              inches (10 to 15 cm) on a side.

              ► A white wall or other white surface (white
                posterboard works well).

              ► A partner.

Assembly

No assembly needed.

To Do and Notice
(15 minutes or more)

Sit so that the white surface or wall is on your right. Hold the bottom of the mirror with your left hand, and put the mirror edge against your nose so that the reflecting surface of the mirror faces sideways, toward the white surface.

While keeping the mirror edge against your nose, rotate the mirror so that your right eye sees just the reflection of the white wall, while your left eye looks forward at the face of a friend who is sitting a couple of feet away (see diagram). Move your hand in front of the white surface as if passing a blackboard eraser over the surface. Watch as parts of your friend's face disappear.

It will help if your friend is sitting very still against a plain, light-colored background. You should also try to keep your own head as still as possible.

If you have trouble seeing your friend's face disappear, one of your eyes might be stronger than the other. Try the experiment again, but this time switch the eye you use to look at the person and the eye you use to look at the wall.

Individuals vary greatly in their ability to perceive this effect; a few people may never succeed in observing it. You may have to try this several times. Don't give up too soon! Give yourself time to see the effect.

What's Going On?

Normally, your two eyes see very slightly different pictures of the world around you. Your brain analyzes these two pictures and then combines them to create a single, three-dimensional image.

In this Snack, the mirror lets your eyes see two very different views. One eye looks straight ahead at another person, while the other eye looks at the white wall or screen and your moving hand. Your brain tries to put together a picture that makes sense by selecting bits and pieces from both views.

Your brain is very sensitive to changes and motion. Since the other person is sitting very still, your brain emphasizes the information coming from the moving hand, and parts of the person's face disappear. No one knows how or why parts of the face sometimes remain, but the eyes and the mouth seem to be the last features to disappear. The lingering mouth gives rise to the name of this exhibit.

○ ○ ○ ○ ○ ○   **etc.**   ○ ○ ○ ○ ○ ○

The name for this exhibit derives from the Cheshire Cat in Lewis Carroll's story *Alice's Adventures in Wonderland.* The cat disappears, leaving behind only its smile.

Color Contrast

A colored object may look different against different-colored backgrounds.

▶ From this experiment, you can see how colors seem to change when you place them against different backgrounds. You need to consider this phenomenon when you pick out colors for carpeting or walls, or when you are painting a picture.

Materials ▸ Construction or origami paper in the following colors: yellow, purple, green, blue (two shades), and orange (two shades). Select pieces of paper of the same size.

▸ Paint sample cards (from paint or hardware stores) that show gradations of one color.

▸ Glue.

Assembly
(15 minutes or less)

Cut one sheet of orange paper in half and glue it to cover up half of a blue sheet. This gives you a large sheet of paper that is half blue and half orange. This large piece of paper will be your background for other colors.

Cut two small squares from each of the colors you have, including squares of blue or orange of a different shade than the large sheets. Glue these squares across from each other, one on

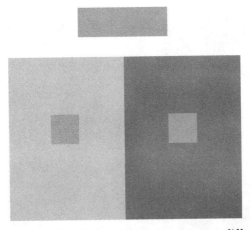

This illustration shows two identical sample squares on two different backgrounds, and a comparison bar.

the blue background and one on the orange background. From the same colors as the small squares, cut strips of each color as wide as the sides of the square to use for comparison.

To Do and Notice
(15 minutes or more)

Notice that two small squares of the same color may appear to be different shades when they are mounted on differing backgrounds. Place the comparison strip so that it touches both small squares of color at the same time to verify that the squares are actually the same color. Experiment with different colors to see which background colors make foreground colors appear lighter and which make them appear darker.

Color contrast also works in reverse: against certain backgrounds, different colors can look the same. From the paint samples, choose two shades that are very similar but are clearly distinguishable when placed right next to each other. Put the paint samples on different backgrounds. The slightly different colors may then appear to be the same. You will have to experiment with different backgrounds to get the desired effect.

What's Going On?

The back of your eye is lined with light-sensitive cells, including color-sensitive *cone* cells. Your cones affect each other in complex ways. These connections give you good color vision, but they can also fool your eye.

When cones in one part of your eye see blue light, they make nearby cones less sensitive to blue. Because of this, you see a colored spot on a blue background as less blue than it really is. If you put a purple spot on a blue background, for instance, the spot looks a little less blue than it would otherwise. Similarly, a red spot on an orange background looks less orange than it would otherwise.

Of course, your eye can't remove any colors from a spot if the colors aren't there in the first place. A yellow spot doesn't appear to change colors against a blue background, because yellow doesn't contain any blue.

○ ○ ○ ○ ○ ○ **etc.** ○ ○ ○ ○ ○ ○ ○

When nineteenth-century astronomers observed Mars through telescopes, they saw a wave of green spread down from the planet's north pole as the polar cap disappeared each spring. Modern astronomers know that this wave of green is actually a wave of gray volcanic dust spread by carbon dioxide expanding from the dry ice of the polar cap. A red background makes gray spots look greenish. The gray dust of Mars appeared green to human eyes when it was viewed against the planet's red background.

Depth Spinner

What happens when you get off the merry-go-round?

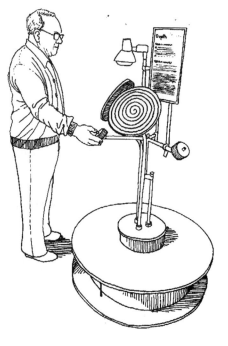

▶ Your eyes' motion detectors are fatigued when you watch a rotating spiral. When you look away, the world seems to move toward or away from you.

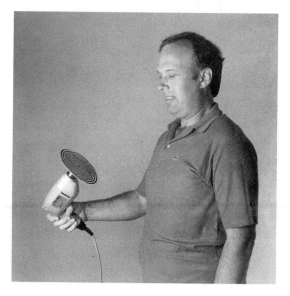

Materials ▸ Cardboard.

▸ Glue or tape.

▸ Pattern disk (included here).

▸ Access to a copy machine.

▸ Rotator (record player, portable beater, variable-speed electric drill, hand drill, etc.).

▸ Optional: adhesive-backed Velcro™.

▸ Adult help.

Assembly
(15 minutes or less)

Make a copy of the pattern disk. Cut the pattern out and mount it on a circle of cardboard with glue or tape. Attach the disk at its center to a rotator. Old phonograph players that spin at 45 or 78 rpm are great for this. Adhesive-backed Velcro™ can be used to secure the disk to a variable-speed electric drill. The drill may also be reversed.

To Do and Notice
(5 minutes or more)

Start the spiral rotating and stare at its center for about 15 seconds.

Look away from the disk and stare at a wall or a nearby person. Notice that the wall or person seems to be expanding or contracting, like he or she is rushing toward you or away from you.

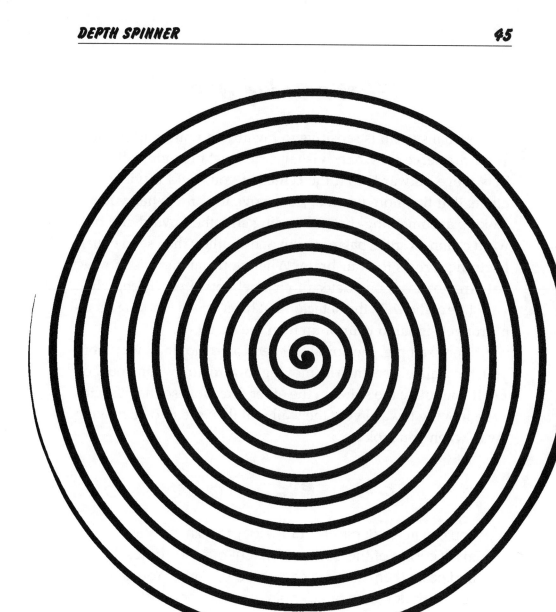

If you can, try rotating the spiral in the opposite direction. Now what happens when you look up from the spinning pattern?

What's Going On?

Your visual system is sensitive to inward and outward motion. There are nerve cells in the visual cortex that fire more when objects move outward from the center of your field of view, and others that fire more when objects move inward. When you are looking at something that is standing still, the inward and outward channels are in balance with one another; they send equally strong signals to your brain. When you stare at this moving pattern, however, one detector channel gets tired. Then, when you stare at the wall, the detector that hasn't been working sends a stronger signal to your brain than the tired one.

If, for example, the spiral seemed to be moving away from you, the wall will seem to be moving toward you when you look up. If you rotate the spiral in the other direction, so that it seems to be moving toward you, the wall will then seem to be moving away when you look up.

○ ○ ○ ○ ○ ○ **etc.** ○ ○ ○ ○ ○ ○

You can make duplicates of the depth spinner. Make many copies of the pattern disk. Cut out the copies and paste them on small cardboard backings. You can spin your disk on a pencil point or a pin, or attach a disk to a pencil eraser with a pushpin.

Next time you are near a waterfall, try staring at one point of the waterfall for a minute. Then look at a rock or another stationary object to the side of the waterfall. The solid object will seem to flow upward. This apparent motion is due to the fatigue of the channels in your visual system that detect linear upward and downward motion.

Disappearing Act

If you want to stay hidden, you'd better stay still.

▶ Some animals blend in with their surroundings so well that they're nearly impossible to see. Only when these animals move can you detect their presence and shape. With this Snack, you can compare what you see when a camouflaged figure remains still to what you see when the figure is moving.

Materials ▶ 2 pieces of dark blue or black construction paper.

▶ Liquid correction fluid.

▶ A piece of clear plastic the same size as the construction paper.

▶ A partner.

Assembly
(30 minutes or less)

Cut out an animal shape from one of the pieces of paper. Leave a projecting rectangle of paper to serve as a handle (see photo).

Use correction fluid to make a random pattern of dots on both the animal figure and the second piece of paper. The second piece of paper will act as the background for the figure.

Place the figure on the background and cover both pieces of paper with the plastic. The transparent covering keeps the edges of the animal flat against the background.

To Do and Notice
(5 minutes or more)

View the animal cutout against the background from an arm's length away. It should be very difficult, if not impossible, to detect the shape of the animal. If you can see the edges, move about 6 feet (2 m) away and have a friend hold the animal and the background.

Place the cutout so that you can use the handle to move the animal while it is under the glass or plastic. Notice that this movement makes it easy to detect the presence of the animal and to identify its shape.

By making several different shapes you can make a game of this. Can anyone identify the animal before it moves? Who can identify it first when it moves?

What's Going On?

Many animals have patterns of color on their bodies that allow them to blend into the background. These animals are hard to detect when they're still. But when the animals move, you can easily pick them out. That's because humans, as well as many other animals, have specialized brain cells that detect motion. These cells receive information from the light-sensitive cells at the back of the eye.

What animals can you think of that use camouflage to blend into their environment?

Everyone Is You and Me

See yourself become someone else.

▶ You and a partner sit on opposite sides of a "two-way" mirror. You vary the amount of light illuminating your face while your partner varies the amount of light illuminating his or her face. As you adjust the light, you will see yourself gradually assume aspects of your partner's features, so that your image becomes a "composite" person.

Materials ▶ A piece of ordinary window glass, approximately 1 × 1 foot (30 × 30 cm).

▶ Aluminized Mylar™ reflecting film to cover one side of the glass. (You can buy this at
most hardware or do-it-yourself stores.)

▶ 2 goose-neck desk lamps.

▶ 2 dimmer switches. (Ready-to-use types
are available at hardware stores. No wiring
is necessary. The configuration used in the
photo requires two adapters. See the diagram.)

▶ 2 extension cords.

▶ Mirror stand of some sort. (There are any
number of ways to stand the glass up; see
the Assembly section.)

▶ A partner. Adult help.

Assembly
(1 hour or less)

You can make a two-way mirror from inexpensive Mylar™ reflecting film and ordinary window glass. The variable illumina-
tion is accomplished with dimmers commonly available at hardware stores.

To make a two-way mirror, put the reflecting film on one side
of the glass, following the instructions for the particular brand
of film used. Cover the edges of the glass with cloth tape to pre-
vent the film from peeling and to avoid cuts from any sharp
edges on the glass.

Place the lamps as shown in the diagram below. Connect each lamp to a dimmer switch and an extension cord.

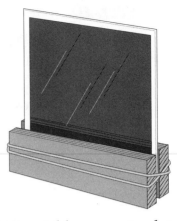

Stand the mirror on a table. This may be done by standing the mirror between two heavy masses (such as 2 pound [1 kg] lab masses), or by making a wooden stand of some sort. A "sandwich" of two pieces of wood with the mirror in the middle, all rubber-banded together, will work. If you have a table saw, cut a slot for the mirror in a piece of wood. Anything that works will do.

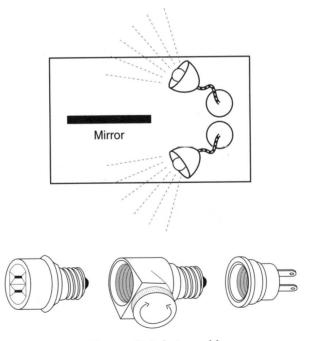

Dimmer Switch Assembly

To Do and Notice
(15 minutes or more)

Sit across the table from your partner with the two-way mirror in between. The room should be dimly lit or dark. Be sure that you and your partner are the same distance from the mirror. You should be able to see both your partner's face through the mirror and your own face reflected in the mirror. Line up your reflected eyes and nose so that they coincide with your partner's. You will have to adjust your distance from the mirror as you do this. Point one lamp directly at your face and have your partner point the other lamp directly at his or her face. Adjust both lamps so they are initially very dim. Now use the dimmer to vary the amount of light reaching your face. Have your partner adjust his or her dimmer. Watch your features blend with your partner's features.

What's Going On?

The mirror reflects about half of the light that hits it and transmits the other half. If your lamp is dim, there's not much light to bounce off your face and reach the two-way mirror, and your reflection will be dim. If your lamp is dim at the same time your partner's is brightly illuminated, then light from him or her will be transmitted through the two-way mirror and you will see his or her features clearly. As you make your lamp brighter and your partner makes his or her lamp dimmer, you will see more of your own features and less of your partner's. Your brain combines the two images into one perceived face.

Fading Dot

Now you see it; now you don't. An object without a sharp edge can fade from your view.

▶ A fuzzy, colored dot that has no distinct edges seems to disappear. As you stare at the dot, its color appears to blend with the colors surrounding it.

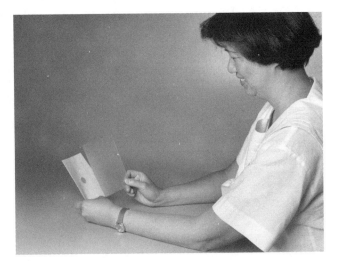

Materials ▸ Pink paper (1 sheet).

▸ Blue paper dot (about 1 inch [2.5 cm] in diameter).

▸ Waxed paper.

Assembly
(5 minutes or less)

Use the blue paper to make a 1 inch (2.5 cm) dot, and place the dot in the center of the pink paper. Cover the paper with a sheet of waxed paper. Look through the waxed paper at the colored papers below. Lift the waxed paper from the pink paper until you see very faint blue color in a field of pale pink.

To Do and Notice
(5 minutes or more)

Stare at a point next to the fuzzy dot for a while without moving your eyes or your head. The blue will gradually fade into the field of pink. As soon as you move your head or eyes, notice that the dot reappears. Experiment with other color combinations.

What's Going On?

Even though you are not aware of it, your eyes are always making tiny jittering movements. Each time your eyes move, they receive new information and send it to your brain. You need this constant new information to see images.

Your eyes also jitter when you look at this dot, but the color changes at the edge of the dot (as seen fuzzily through the waxed paper) are so gradual that your eyes can't tell the difference between one point on the dot and a point right next to it. Your eyes receive no new information, and the image seems to fade away. If the dot had a distinct border, your eyes would immediately detect the change when they jittered, and you would continue to see the dot.

You may have noticed that, although the dot fades, just about everything else in your field of vision remains clear. That's because everything else you see has distinct edges.

○ ○ ○ ○ ○ ○ **etc.** ○ ○ ○ ○ ○ ○

For more information, we suggest you read the sections on lateral inhibition and chromatic lateral inhibition in *Seeing the Light,* by David Falk, Dieter Brill, and David Stork (Harper & Row, 1986).

Far Out Corners

Your experience of the world influences what you see.

► When they first glance at this exhibit, many people say, "What's the big deal? It's just a bunch of boxes." But there are no boxes at all. A closer look reveals that the **Far Out Corners** *exhibit is a cluster of corners lit from below. When you walk past the exhibit with one eye closed, the cubes will seem to turn mysteriously so that they follow your movement.*

Materials ► A large cardboard box measuring about 19 × 15 inches (48 × 38 cm).

► Flat black spray paint.

► Thick, white, nonflexible posterboard measuring at least 15 × 15 inches (38 × 38 cm).

► X-Acto™ knife or matte knife.

► Masking tape or transparent tape.

► A bright free-standing lamp.

► Adult help.

Assembly
(1 hour or less)

You can cut the inside corners from square-cornered containers, such as clean milk cartons or tissue boxes, or you can make your own corners from posterboard. To make your own, use an X-Acto™ knife or matte knife to cut the posterboard into nine squares, each of which measures 5 × 5 inches (13 × 13 cm).

Now use three of the squares to construct a partial cube or corner in the following fashion: Tape two squares together at one edge; open each of the two squares into a right angle; tape the

third square on top of the first two squares. Make three partial cubes, or corners.

Spray-paint the inside of the large cardboard box black. When the box is dry, arrange the corners so that two are side by side on the bottom of the box, as shown. Make sure the hollow, open sides of each corner are facing out toward you and down. Tape them so they are tilted up at a small angle. Place the third corner as far forward as possible on top of the original two, also tilted upward. Tape all three corners in place. Now position the light so that it shines directly into the box.

To Do and Notice
(15 minutes or more)

Stand back ten feet and close one eye. With a little mental effort, you can see the corners that you have constructed as three-dimensional cubes rather than hollow corners.

Walk back and forth parallel to the box. Notice that the cube on top seems to be following you as you move.

What's Going On?

The first step to successfully seeing the top partial cube turn with you lies in your ability to perceive it as a complete six-sided figure. This perception has a lot to do with being raised in a society that recognizes cubes as a common shape. Your brain is used to seeing cubes, so it fills in the rest of the cube shape, even though this partial cube only has three sides.

As you move past the exhibit, your view of the corners changes in a way that would not make any sense if the corners were stationary cubes. Your eye–brain system is used to seeing things that are near you move faster than things that are farther away. When you are riding in a car, for example, nearby objects seem to whiz by, whereas distant objects seem to follow you at a slower pace. Since you perceive this inside corner to be the outside of a solid cube, your brain "sees" the corner farthest from you as being the closest. To maintain this misconception, your brain perceives a rapid rotation of the cube as your angle to the corner changes.

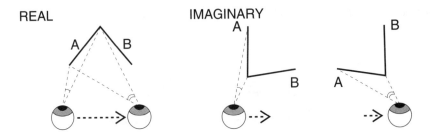

The diagram above shows how this illusion works. In the real situation, as your eye moves to the right, it sees more of side A. In order to see more of side A of the imagined corner, the perceived cube must be seen to rotate as you move.

Gray Step

Without a boundary, it's hard to distinguish different shades of gray.

▶ You can't believe all that you see. Two slightly different shades of the same color may look different if there is a sharp boundary between them. But if the boundary is obscured, the two shades may be indistinguishable.

Materials ▸ A sheet of Pantone™ 404 u-g graduated paper, uncoated (available at art supply stores
in 20 × 24 inch sheets).

  ▸ Cardboard or masonite.

  ▸ A "horse tail" made of a length of hanging
  yarn, twine, or rope.

  ▸ A sheet of white paper.

  ▸ A hole punch.

  ▸ Scissors or paper cutter.

  ▸ Glue or tape.

  ▸ Adult help.

Assembly
(30 minutes or less)

You can use the image provided on page 61 or make your own
gray step by following these instructions.

Punch two holes 4 inches (10 cm) apart near the edge of a
sheet of white paper and set it aside.

Put the large sheet of graduated paper in front of you with
the dark side to the *left*. Cut a strip 2 inches (5 cm) wide from the
right side of the paper (the lightest side). Throw this strip away.

Now cut a 4 inch (10 cm) wide strip from the *new* right side.
Cut this piece in half so that you have two shorter but identical
pieces.

Place the light side of one piece next to the dark side of its
twin. Mount the pieces on cardboard or masonite with glue or
tape. Attach the horse tail above the boundary between the two
pieces so that it hangs down and covers the boundary.

To Do and Notice
(5 minutes or more)

In this Snack, a fuzzy cord (the "horse tail") is used to obscure the boundary between two gray areas. You see one uniform gray area when the horse tail is in place, and two different gray areas when the horse tail is removed. But you never see the truth: Both gray areas are really identical to each other and grade from light gray at one edge to dark gray at the other. In general, your brain ignores slight gradations in gray level.

If you are using the image in this book, just place a pencil or your finger over the boundary between the gray halves. What do you see? If you are using your own construction, position the horse tail so that it covers the boundary and ask your friends what they see. Most people will see a uniformly gray piece of paper with a rope hanging down the middle.

Lift the tail and ask again. Most people will see two uniform areas, each a different shade of gray.

To show that the two sides are identically shaded areas, hold the punched piece of paper over the gray areas, with one hole on each side of the boundary. The two areas viewed through the punches will always be the same shade of gray.

What's Going On?

Actually, the two rectangles are exactly the same. At the right edge both rectangles are light gray. Both become darker toward the left. Where the rectangles meet, the dark part of one rectangle contrasts sharply with the light part of the other, so you see a distinct edge. When the edge is covered, however, the two regions look the same uniform shade of gray.

It is difficult to distinguish between different shades of gray or shades of the same color if there is no sharp edge between them. This is true even though a sensitive light meter would show that the different shades are reflecting different amounts of light to your eyes. Your eyes do not lack the necessary sensitivity to detect the difference: if there is an edge between the two shades, the difference is obvious.

Your eye–brain system, however, condenses the information it obtains from more than a hundred million light-detecting rods and cones in the retina in order to send the information over a million neurons to your brain. Your eye–brain system enhances the ratio of reflected light at edges. If one region of the retina is stimulated by light, lateral connections turn down the sensitivity of adjacent regions. This is called *lateral inhibition.* Conversely, if one region is in the dark, the sensitivity of adjacent regions is increased. This means that a dark region next to a light region looks even darker, and vice versa. As a result, your visual system is most sensitive to changes in brightness and color.

When the horse tail is absent and the normal boundary is visible, lateral inhibition enhances the contrast between the two shades of gray. The bright side appears brighter and the dark side darker. When the tail is in place, the boundary between the two different grays is spread apart across the retina so that it no longer falls on adjacent regions. Lateral inhibition then does not help us distinguish between the different shades, and the eye–brain system judges them to be the same.

○ ○ ○ ○ ○ ○   **etc.**   ○ ○ ○ ○ ○ ○

Another easy *Gray Step* demonstration can be constructed out of paint sample pieces from the hardware store. Some paint brands provide good-sized individual color chips. Experiment with how different two colors can be and yet appear the same when the boundary between them is obscured.

A good source of background reading is *Seeing the Light* by David Falk, Dieter Brill, and David Stork (Harper & Row, 1986).

Jacques Cousteau in Seashells

There's more to seeing than meets the eye!

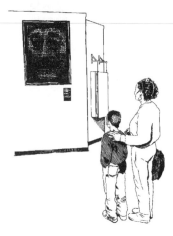

▶ Seeing is a cooperative effort involving your eyes and your brain. Your eyes may perceive a group of dots, but it is your brain that has to decide whether the dots form a pattern that means something. In the exhibit "Jacques Cousteau in Seashells," created for the Exploratorium by artist Ken Knowlton, a framed collection of seashells seems to be a random pattern when viewed up close. At a distance, however, the pattern is seen to be a likeness of well-known oceanographer Jacques Cousteau.

Materials ▸ Graph paper with ¼ inch (6 mm) squares.

▸ A black-and-white picture.

▸ A pencil.

▸ Paper clips.

Assembly
(30 minutes or less)

You can use the pattern of dots supplied here for the To Do and Notice section, or you can make your own dot pattern. If you choose to make your own, you will need a black-and-white photograph of a simple, easily recognizable scene or person. (You could even use a picture of Jacques Cousteau!) You can translate this photo into a pattern of dots by following these steps:

1. Place graph paper on top of the photo. Paper clip the picture to the graph paper so it will stay in the same place while you are drawing.

2. Notice that dark portions of the photo show through the graph paper. Pick a square to start your drawing from. Estimate what portion of the square is black. Draw a dot whose size corresponds to the percentage of black you estimate is in the square—the more black in the square, the bigger your dot; see the diagram on page 69. If the square is not black but rather some shade of gray, the size of the dot will depend on how dark the gray is. In a square filled with pale gray, put a small dot; in a square filled with dark gray, put a bigger dot.

3. Repeat the process with each square in the picture until you are finished.

To Do and Notice
(5 minutes or more)

For simplicity, a picture of an eye is used in this Snack activity in place of the image of Jacques Cousteau.

Hold the dot picture at arm's length. If the dot picture is of a familiar object, it should be easily recognizable at this distance. See if other people can identify the object in the picture.

Unfamiliar or complicated objects may be more difficult to recognize at close range. Place the picture across the room, and you'll notice that it becomes much easier to recognize. The dots in the picture seem to disappear, and only the pattern remains. The picture may appear slightly fuzzy, but it certainly doesn't appear to be made of dots!

What's Going On?

Pictures made of dots are easily recognized by the brain because the brain is always attempting to interpret what it sees. Even though the picture of the eye in this Snack is made up of different-sized dots, the brain recognizes the overall shape as that of an eye, since it is very familiar with that shape. This is the same reason a person may see shapes in clouds or inkblots. The brain does not merely register these shapes as abstract patterns, but attempts to interpret them based on previous experience.

The dots disappear when you view the picture from a distance because of the limited resolving power of your eyes. You see the dot picture because light reflecting from the page makes an image on the retina of your eye. This image stimulates the light-sensitive cells in the retina and your brain interprets the result. When you move the dot picture farther away from your eye, the image the picture makes on your retina becomes smaller. The images of the dots overlap on the light-sensitive cells. Unable to distinguish between adjacent dots, your eye perceives shades of gray, rather than black dots and white spaces.

If the picture looks like this... ...your dot would look like this.

25%
50%
75%
100%

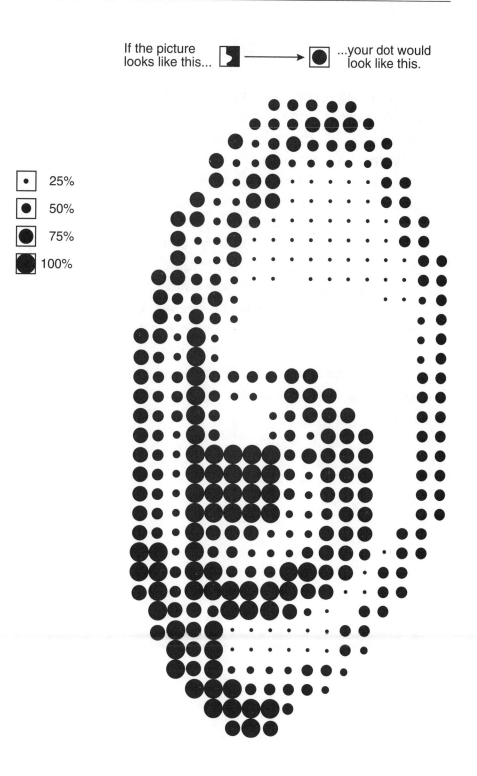

○ ○ ○ ○ ○ ○   **etc.**   ○ ○ ○ ○ ○ ○

To print shades of gray using black ink on white paper, printers use "halftone" reproduction. The phenomenon of the "disappearing" dots is the basis of these halftones. A magnifying glass will show you that printed photos in newspapers, books, and magazines are actually composed of thousands of tiny dots, often too small for the eye to separate.

Artists in the late nineteenth century, taking advantage of this phenomenon, created a style called Pointillism. Paintings in this style—most notably those by Georges Seurat (1859–91)—are made up of thousands of tiny dots of brilliant color that, at a distance, merge in the beholder's eye.

The picture on a color TV set is also made up of dots. Your eye blends these dots to make a picture.

Mirrorly a Window

What you see is often affected by what you expect to see.

▶ When your brain expects to see one thing and is presented with something quite different, you will feel some peculiar sensations.

Materials ▸ 2 mirrors, 12 × 12 inches (30 × 30 cm), either glass mirror tiles or plastic mirrors.

▸ 2 wooden dowels, 1 inch (2.5 cm) in diameter × 1 foot (30 cm) long.

▸ Epoxy glue.

▸ Duct tape.

▸ Optional: dowel screw.

▸ Adult help.

Assembly
(15 minutes plus time for glue to dry)

Glue the mirrors together, back to back. If you are using glass mirror tiles, tape the sharp edges—be careful! Broken glass is dangerous! Glue a wooden dowel to each mirror. The dowel should be positioned so that it sticks straight out of the middle of the mirror.

For a more durable assembly, use plastic mirrors and a dowel screw. This is a double-ended screw used to join two dowels. Drill a hole in the mirror and a hole in the end of each dowel. Insert the dowel in the mirror hole and screw on the dowels until tight.

To Do and Notice
(5 minutes or more)

Grab a dowel with each hand. While looking at one side of the mirror, move the hand on the other side of the mirror.

What's Going On?

Your brain is fooled into thinking that the image it sees in the mirror is actually your other hand. When you move that hand, your brain naturally expects to see the hand move. After all, messages from the nerves in that hand tell your brain that the hand is moving. The hand's apparent failure to move is profoundly disturbing to your brain, which doesn't enjoy having its assumptions trifled with!

○ ○ ○ ○ ○ ○   **etc.**   ○ ○ ○ ○ ○ ○

A simpler version of this experiment uses a single 12 × 12 inch (30 cm) mirror with no epoxied handles. Prop the mirror up on a table. Hold one of your arms on each side of the mirror so that you see the reflection of one arm as the continuation of the other arm. Snap the fingers on both your hands simultaneously, then stop snapping the fingers on only one hand. Or have someone drop an object (such as a set of keys) into the hand behind the mirror.

Moiré Patterns

When you overlap materials with repetitive lines, you create moiré patterns.

▶ When you look through one chain-link fence at another, you sometimes see a pattern of light and dark lines that shifts as you move. This pattern, called a **moiré pattern,** *appears when two repetitive patterns overlap. Moiré patterns are created whenever one semitransparent object with a repetitive pattern is placed over another. A slight motion of one of the objects creates large-scale changes in the moiré pattern. These patterns can be used to demonstrate wave interference.*

Materials ► 2 identical pocket combs, or a pocket comb and a mirror.

► 2 pieces of window screen, or a window screen, a sheet of white cardboard, and a bright light.

► Access to a copy machine.

► 2 transparencies made from the pattern provided in this Snack. (See Etc. for other suggestions.)

► Optional: Moiré patterns are commercially available from the Exploratorium Store in the form of plastic bags decorated with repetitive patterns, in the book *Seeing the Light* (a shimmer pattern is on page 259), in *The Moving Pattern Book,* and in the *Kaleidograph* set.

Assembly

No assembly is needed.

To Do and Notice
(15 minutes or more)

Hold two identical combs so that one is directly in front of the other and they are about a finger-width apart. Look through the teeth and notice the patterns of light and dark that appear. This is a moiré pattern. Slide the combs from side to side and watch the moiré pattern move. Now rotate one comb relative to the other and notice how the pattern changes.

If you only have one comb, hold it at arm's length, about 1 inch (2.5 cm) from a mirror. Look through the comb at its reflection in the mirror. Notice how the moiré pattern moves when you move the comb to the side or slowly tip one end away from the mirror.

Look through two layers of window screen. Observe the moiré patterns as you slide one layer from side to side across the other, or when you rotate one layer. You can also create interesting patterns by flexing one of the screens.

If you only have one piece of screen, you can still make moiré patterns—even if the screen is still mounted in a window or a door. Have a friend hold a sheet of white cardboard behind the screen, and shine a single bright light onto the screen. (On a sunny day, sunshine can serve as your light source.) Start with the cardboard touching the screen, then move it away, tilting the cardboard a little as you go. The screen will form a moiré pattern with its own shadow. Replace the cardboard with flexible white paper and bend the paper. Notice how the pattern changes.

Use a copy machine to make two transparencies from the pattern of concentric circles provided with this Snack. Look through these two patterns as you move them apart and then together. The moiré pattern consists of radiating dark and light lines.

You can project moiré patterns so that a large group can see them. Just make two transparencies of a repetitive pattern and overlap the transparencies on an overhead projector. Moiré patterns from books may be enlarged or reduced and made into transparencies on a copy machine.

What's Going On?

When two identical repetitive patterns of lines, circles, or arrays of dots are overlapped with imperfect alignment, the pattern of

light and dark lines that we call a *moiré pattern* appears. The moiré pattern is not a pattern in the screens themselves, but rather a pattern in the image formed in your eye. In some places, black lines on the front screen hide the clear lines on the rear screen, creating a dark area. Where the black lines on the front screen align with black lines on the rear, the neighboring clear areas show through, leaving a light region. The patterns formed by the regions of dark and light are moiré patterns.

In the case of the two sets of concentric circular lines, the dark lines are like the nodal lines of a two-source interference pattern. A typical two-source interference pattern is created when light passes through two slits. Along lines known as *nodal lines,* the peaks of the light waves from one slit and the valleys of the light waves from the other slit overlap and cancel each other. No light is detected along a nodal line.

In the black radiating lines of the moiré pattern, the black lines of one moiré pattern fill the transparent lines of the other. Note that as the patterns are moved apart, the dark, nodal lines move together. This is the same thing that happens when light passes through two slits and the slits are moved farther apart.

Moiré patterns magnify differences between two repetitive patterns. If two patterns are exactly lined up, then no moiré pattern appears. The slightest misalignment of two patterns will create a large-scale, easily visible moiré pattern. As the misalignment increases, the lines of the moiré pattern will appear thinner and closer together.

○ ○ ○ ○ ○ ○   **etc.**   ○ ○ ○ ○ ○ ○

Once you have learned to see moiré patterns, you'll begin to see them practically everywhere. Look through two chain-link fences and notice the pattern.

Watch it shift as you drive by. Look through a thin, finely woven fabric, such as a white handkerchief, or some pantyhose material. Now fold the fabric over and look again through two layers. You'll see moiré patterns. Slide the fabric around and watch the patterns dance and change.

Peripheral Vision

We are not usually aware of our eyes' limitations.

▶ This Snack is basically a large protractor that lets you test the limits of your **peripheral vision**. With the help of a friend, you can measure how much you can see out of the corner of your eye. You will find that you can detect motion at a wide angle, colors at a narrow angle, and detailed shapes at a surprisingly narrow angle.

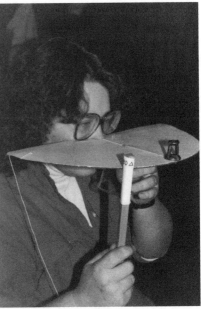

Materials ▶ Posterboard, cardboard, foamcore, or other stiff material, 1 × 2 feet (30 × 60 cm).

▶ A pushpin to use initially in drawing a circle, and finally as a point of reference.

▶ A pencil.

▶ Scissors.

▶ 1 piece of string about 2 feet (60 cm) long.

▶ A small plastic cup.

▶ One 6 inch (15 cm) length of 1 × 1 inch (2.5 cm × 2.5 cm) wood or a few 3 × 5 inch (8 × 13 cm) file cards.

▶ Glue.

▶ Marking pens in different colors.

▶ A partner.

Assembly
(30 minutes or less)

Stick the pushpin, point down, halfway along the 2 foot (60 cm) edge of the posterboard (or whatever board you use as a base). Tie the pencil to one end of the string, and wrap the other end of the string around the pushpin to improvise a compass. Draw a half-circle with a 1 foot (30 cm) radius. Now shorten the string and draw another, smaller half-circle, about ¾ inch (2 cm) in diameter. Cut these both out (see the diagram on page 82). The small circle should be just big enough for your nose.

Now stick the pushpin in at the edge of the half-circle, directly across from the nose hole. This will be your focus object.

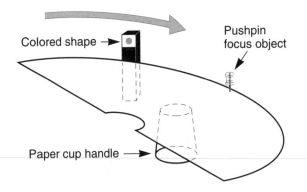

Use glue to attach the plastic cup to the bottom of the poster-board. The cup will serve as a handle.

Use the marking pens to draw simple shapes (such as rectangles, squares, and triangles), each in a different color, on the faces at one end of the length of wood, or on the file cards. This will allow you to reveal only one shape at a time.

To Do and Notice
(15 minutes or more)

Using the cup as a handle, hold the posterboard base up to your face and put your nose in the center hole. Have your partner hold the wood or file card so that it is against the curved side of the base, as far from the focus object as possible. Keep your eyes on the focus object while your partner moves the colored shape around the outside edge until you can see it. Note the angle.

Have your partner keep moving the colored shape toward the focus object. Note the angle at which you first detect color. Then note the angle at which you first discern the shape itself. Have your partner expose a different shape and repeat the experiment. You'll probably find that your partner has to move the wood surprisingly close to the focus object before you can make out color or shape.

What's Going On?

Your *retina*—the light-sensitive lining at the back of your eye—is packed with light-receiving cells called *rods* and *cones*. Only the cones are sensitive to color. These cells are clustered mainly in the central region of the retina.

When you see something out of the corner of your eye, its image focuses on the periphery of your retina, where there are few cones. Thus, it isn't surprising that you can't distinguish the color of something you see out of the corner of your eye.

The rods are more evenly spread across the retina, but they also become less densely packed toward the outer regions of the retina. Because there are fewer rods, you have a limited ability to resolve the shapes of objects at the periphery of your vision.

In the center of your field of view is a region in which the cones are packed tightly together. This region is called the *fovea*. This region, which is surprisingly small, gives you the sharpest view of an object. The fraction of your eye covered by the fovea is about the same as the fraction of the night sky covered by the moon.

You can demonstrate this effect more simply by focusing on one of the words on this page while at the same time trying to make out other words to the right or left. You may be able to make out a word or two, depending on how far the page is from your eyes. But the area that you can see clearly is the area imaged on the fovea of your eye.

Generally, you are not aware of the limitations of your peripheral vision. You think that you have a clear view of the world because your eyes are always in motion. Wherever you look, you see a sharp, clear image.

Interestingly, your peripheral vision is very sensitive to motion—a characteristic that probably had strong adaptive value during the earlier stages of human evolution.

○ ○ ○ ○ ○ ○ **etc.** ○ ○ ○ ○ ○ ○

You almost always need an assistant to do this Snack. As the colored shape approaches the center of your field of view, the temptation to cheat and move your eyes to look at the object becomes nearly irresistible. An assistant can watch you, and stop the experiment when you give in to temptation and move your eyes to look.

Persistence of Vision

Your eye and brain hold on to a series of images to form a single complete picture.

▶ When you look through a narrow slit, you can see only a thin strip of the world around you. But if you move the slit around rapidly, your eye and brain combine these thin strips to make a single complete picture.

Materials ▸ A cardboard mailing tube about 3 inches (8 cm) in diameter and 2 to 3 feet (60 to 90 cm) long, with a cap over one end.

▸ A sharp knife.

▸ Adult help.

Assembly
(5 minutes or less)

With a knife, cut a slit in the cap of the mailing tube. The slit should be about 1 inch (2.5 cm) long and ⅛ inch (3 mm) wide. Replace the cap on the end of the tube.

To Do and Notice
(5 minutes or more)

Close one eye. Put the other eye to the open end of the tube. Cup your hand around the tube to make a cushion between the tube and your eye. Hold the tube so that the slit is vertical.

When the slit is stationary, you can't see much. Keep your head and body still and sweep the far end of the tube back and forth slowly while you look through it. Increase the scanning speed and compare the views. Notice that when you sweep the tube quickly from side to side, you can obtain a rather clear view of your surroundings.

What's Going On?

Your eye and brain retain a visual impression for about ⅓₀th of a second. (The exact time depends on the brightness of the image.) This ability to retain an image is known as *persistence of vision*. As you swing the tube from side to side, the eye is presented with a succession of narrow, slit-shaped images. When you move the tube fast enough, your brain retains the images long enough to build up a complete image of your surroundings.

Persistence of vision accounts for our failure to notice that a motion picture screen is dark about half the time, and that a television image is just one bright, fast, little dot sweeping the screen. Motion pictures show one new frame every ¼₄th of a second. Each frame is shown three times during this period. The eye retains the image of each frame long enough to give us the illusion of smooth motion.

○ ○ ○ ○ ○ ○ **etc.** ○ ○ ○ ○ ○ ○

The *Viking 1* and *2* landers photographed the surface of Mars by recording narrow-slit images that were transmitted to earth and assembled by computer to make the final surface photographs. As this demonstration shows, your eye and brain can "take a photograph" in the same way.

Pupil

Your pupil changes size to control how much light enters your eye.

▶ You can observe that the pupil of your eye changes size in response to changes in lighting. You can also experiment to determine how light shining in one eye affects the size of the pupil in your other eye.

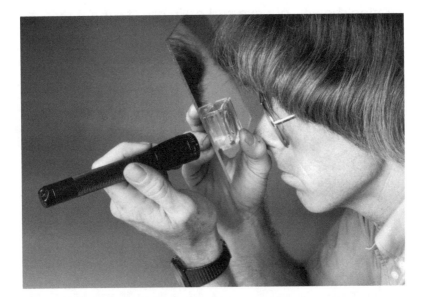

Materials ▸ A magnifying glass (at least 1 inch [2.5 cm] in diameter).

▸ A mirror (a small, flat, compact mirror, a plastic mirror 4 × 4 inches [10 × 10 cm] or larger, or a wall mirror). Plastic mirrors are safer than glass and are available at plastics stores.

▸ A flashlight.

Assembly

No assembly is necessary.

To Do and Notice
(15 minutes or more)

Place the magnifying glass on the surface of the mirror. Look into the center of the magnifying glass with one eye. If you wear contact lenses or glasses, you may either leave them on or remove them. Adjust your distance from the mirror until you see a sharply focused and enlarged image of your eye.

Notice the white of your eye, the colored disk of your iris, and your pupil, the black hole in the center of your iris.

Shine a light into the pupil of one eye. If you are using a small mirror, hold the flashlight behind the mirror and shine the light around the edge of the mirror into your eye. If you are using a large mirror, bounce the flashlight beam off the mirror into your eye. Observe how your pupil changes size.

Notice that it takes longer for your pupil to dilate than it does to contract. Notice also that the pupil sometimes overshoots its mark. You can see it shrink down too far, and then reopen slightly.

Observe changes in the size of one pupil while you, or an assistant, shine a light into and away from the other eye.

In a dimly lit room, open and close one eye while observing the pupil of the other eye in the mirror.

What's Going On?

The pupil is an opening that lets light into your eye. Since most of the light entering your eye does not escape, your pupil appears black. In dim light, your pupil expands to allow more light to enter your eye. In bright light, it contracts. Your pupil can range in diameter from 1.5 millimeters (1/16 of an inch) to more than 8 millimeters (1/3 of an inch).

Light detected by the retina of your eye is converted to nerve impulses that travel down the optic nerve. Some of these nerve impulses go from the optic nerve to the muscles that control the size of the pupil. More light creates more impulses, causing the muscles to close the pupil. Part of the optic nerve from one

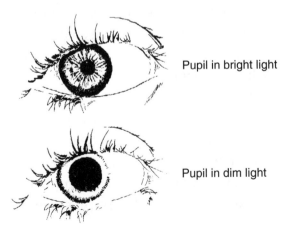

Pupil in bright light

Pupil in dim light

eye crosses over and couples to the muscles that control the pupil size of the other eye. That's why the pupil of one eye can change when you shine the light into your other eye.

In this experiment, the light reflecting from your eye passes through the magnifying lens twice—once on its way to the mirror and once on its way back. Therefore, the image of your eye is magnified twice by the magnifying glass.

○ ○ ○ ○ ○ ○   **etc.**   ○ ○ ○ ○ ○ ○

The size of your pupils actually reflects the state of your body and mind. Pupil size can change because you are fearful, angry, in pain, in love, or under the influence of drugs. Not only does the pupil react to emotional stimuli; it is itself an emotional stimulus. The size of a person's pupils can give another person a strong impression of sympathy or hostility.

The response of the pupil is an involuntary reflex. Like the knee-jerk reflex, the pupillary response is used to test the functions of people who might be ill or injured.

The pupil of your eye is also the source of the red eyes you sometimes see in flash photographs. When the bright light of a camera flash shines directly through the pupil, it can reflect off the red blood of the retina (the light-sensitive lining at the back of your eye), and bounce right back out through the pupil. If this happens, the person in the photograph will appear to have glowing red eyes. To avoid this, photographers move the flash away from the camera lens. With this arrangement, the light from the flash goes through the pupil and illuminates a part of the retina not captured by the camera lens.

Size and Distance

A clueless way to determine the size of an object.

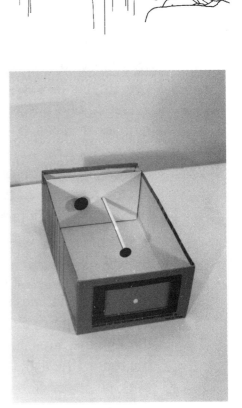

▶ You can trick your brain into thinking that two similar objects of different sizes are really the same size. This is done by removing clues to the actual size and distance of the objects. You can then compare what you see when you limit your information to what you see when you have complete information.

Materials ► A shoe box with lid.

► 2 straws.

► 1 quarter and 1 dime.

► Modeling clay or Fun Tak™ reusable adhesive.

► Construction paper that contrasts with the inside of the shoe box.

► A piece of posterboard or similar-weight cardboard, a little larger than the end of the box.

► A knife or scissors.

► Adult help.

Assembly
(30 minutes or less)

Remove the box lid. At the center of one end-panel of the shoe box, cut a hole large enough for one-eyed viewing (approximately ½ inch [1.3 cm] diameter). Then cut out a window, approximately 3 × 5 inches (8 × 13 cm), with the viewing hole in the center. Replace the cardboard in the window from which it was cut, and tape it in place along its bottom edge to form a hinge inside the box (see the diagram on page 94).

At the other end of the box, make a hole for each straw approximately ½ inch (1.3 cm) to each side of the center of the panel.

Cut the piece of posterboard so that it is the same height as the box and about 2 inches (5 cm) wider than the box. Fold back 1 inch (2.5 cm) on each side to make two flaps. Make two holes in the main portion that coincide exactly with the two holes in

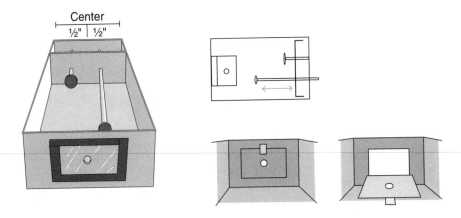

the end of the box. Tape or glue the flaps to the inside sides of the box, using them as spacers to position this piece 1 inch (2.5 cm) from the end with the holes (see diagram).

Insert the straws into the holes. The double set of holes will keep the straws properly aligned.

Using the quarter and dime as templates, cut one circle of each size from the construction paper. Make sure the color of the construction paper contrasts strongly with the color of the inside of the box. Use clay to mount the circles on the ends of the straws inside the box.

To Do and Notice
(15 minutes or more)

With the cover on the box and the hinged window closed, close one eye and look through the viewing hole at the circles. Lift the end of the box cover closest to you and slide it away from you until adequate viewing light reaches the inside of the box. Push or pull on the straws from the outside rear of the box until the mounted circles appear to be the same size. Note that your depth perception is almost nonexistent: both circles look essentially the same distance away, and it is very difficult to judge which circle is closest to you.

Fold the window down and look with both eyes to see the actual positions of the circles. (You may have to move your head back a little from the box to get both circles focused.) Note that depth perception is now a factor and that the circles no longer look the same size or the same distance away.

Position the small disk a couple of inches closer to you than the large disk. With both eyes open, look through the window at the disks. Notice that you have no trouble establishing their size and distance. Now close one eye. You may notice that it is much more difficult to tell whether the small disk is now actually a small disk that's close to you, or a large disk that's far away.

You can also use the dime and quarter by themselves, without building the box, to illustrate the same principle. Close one eye. Holding one coin in each hand, move them toward or away from your viewing eye until they appear to be the same size. A solid-color background gives less distraction than an irregular background. A very bright, solid-colored background works best, so that the coins appear essentially in silhouette and their features cannot be easily distinguished.

What's Going On?

Large, distant objects can appear to be the same size as small, nearby objects. Under normal viewing conditions, with both eyes open, you have the ability to perceive depth. If two objects appear to be the same size, but you know that one is farther away than the other, your brain tells you that the distant object is larger.

When one eye is closed, your depth perception is impaired. In the case of the circles, you can't tell how far away either of the circles really is. Since they are not actually the same size, this means that, for the smaller one to look the same size as the larger one, it will have to be closer to you than the larger one.

With both eyes open, you can gather more information and more points of view, and so you can make more accurate judgments about an object's size, shape, and distance from you.

○ ○ ○ ○ ○ ○ **etc.** ○ ○ ○ ○ ○ ○

There is a pattern on the pupa of the butterfly *Spalgis epius* that looks like the face of a rhesus macaque monkey. Even though the pupa is only half as wide as a human fingernail, it still seems to scare away predatory birds who mistake it for a more distant, and therefore larger, monkey.

Squirming Palm

This visual illusion makes the palm of your hand appear to squirm and twist.

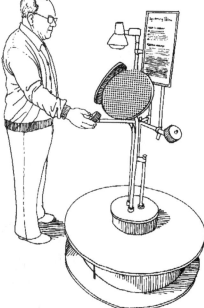

▶ If you stare at a waterfall for some time, and then stare at the rocks nearby, the rocks will appear to be moving upward. This illusion is known as the **waterfall effect.** Using the pattern provided here, you can create the waterfall effect—without getting wet.

Materials ▸ Photocopy of the pattern disk provided.

▸ Cardboard.

▸ Adhesive (glue stick, glue, rubber cement, etc.) or tape.

▸ Access to a copy machine.

▸ Electric or manual rotator. You can use a turntable, a variable-speed electric drill, a portable mixer, an electric screwdriver, or a hand drill. If you prefer a low-tech option, you need a pencil with an eraser on top, and a pushpin or thumbtack.

▸ Adult help if a drill is used.

▸ Optional: adhesive-backed Velcro™.

Assembly
(15 minutes or less)

Cut out the copy of the pattern disk and mount it on cardboard with adhesive or tape.

Attach the disk to some form of rotator. (The adhesive-backed Velcro™ provides a convenient way to mount the disk to a drill or similar device.)

For a low-tech method of rotating the disk, push the pushpin through the center of the pattern into the eraser of a pencil. Spin the disk by hand as you hold the pencil.

To Do and Notice
(5 minutes or more)

Rotate the disk slowly (1 or 2 seconds per revolution) and stare at its center for about 15 seconds. Now look at the palm of your

hand. Notice that your palm seems to be turning. Your palm will turn in the opposite direction from the way the disk was turning.

What's Going On?

Mechanisms in your eye and brain detect motion in various directions. For example, regions of your brain fire nerve impulses when your eye forms images that are rotating in a clockwise direction. Other regions respond to counterclockwise rotation. When something is stationary, both of these motion detectors still fire, but their firing rates are equal. The two signals balance each other out, and you see no motion.

As you stare at the spinning disk, the set of motion detectors that respond to its rotation adapts to the motion of the pattern. These motion detectors start out firing rapidly, and then slowly decrease their firing rate. When you look away from the rotating pattern and stare at a stationary object (such as your palm), the motion detectors that have been firing fire less rapidly than the ones that have not been stimulated. As a result, you see motion in the opposite direction.

You also have sets of motion detectors that respond to upward and downward motion. Adaptation of these upward and downward motion detectors causes the version of the waterfall effect that you notice when you watch a waterfall.

Thread the Needle

Using two eyes gives you depth perception.

▶ Closing one eye eliminates one of the clues that your brain uses to judge depth. Trying to perform a simple task with one eye closed demonstrates how much you rely on your depth perception.

Materials ▶ A dowel or pencil.

▶ A washer with a hole that's a little larger than the dowel's diameter.

▶ A lump of modeling clay about the size of your thumb.

Assembly
(5 minutes or less)

Stand the washer on its side, using the lump of clay to support it so that the edge of the washer—not the hole—is facing you.

To Do and Notice
(5 minutes or more)

Stand far enough from the washer so that you must extend your arm to reach it. Now close one eye and try to put the dowel through the hole in the washer.

Open both eyes and try again.

What's Going On?

One of the clues that your brain uses to judge distance and depth is the very slight difference between what your left eye sees and what your right eye sees. Your brain combines these two views to make a three-dimensional picture of the world.

Try this experiment again with one eye closed. But this time, move your head from side to side as you "thread the needle." People who have lost an eye can learn to perceive depth by comparing the different views they obtain from one eye at two separate times.

○ ○ ○ ○ ○ ○   **etc.**   ○ ○ ○ ○ ○ ○

Stretch a string from just under your nose to the end of your outstretched arm. You will see two strings stretching out in front of you. Look at the string with just your left eye, and then with just your right eye. Notice that the two strings are separate images—one from each eye. The two strings cross at the point on which your eyes are focused. Try looking at different points on the string and notice how the crossover point moves.

Vanna

A face seen upside down may hold some surprises.

▶ Your brain gets used to seeing familiar things in certain ways. When the brain receives a strange view of a familiar object, the consequences can be intriguing. In the Exploratorium exhibit titled "Vanna," two pictures of the face of TV personality Vanna White seem identical when viewed upside down, but exhibit a bizarre difference when viewed right-side up.

Materials ► 3 identical full-page (or at least fairly large) pictures of a familiar face from a magazine. Try cover photos from magazines like *Time, Sports Illustrated, People,* etc. Choose your magazine and picture to suit your audience so that you use personalities who will be known by them. Pictures of a smiling person work exceptionally well. Avoid photos with shadows around the mouth area.

► Posterboard or cardboard for backing.

► A glue stick or other adhesive.

► Scissors.

Assembly
(15 minutes or less)

Cut two pieces of posterboard to the size of the pictures you cut out. If you are using a magazine cover, you can use the whole cover or you can trim off the title. It is not necessary to trim the picture to the outline of the person.

Glue the first picture to a piece of posterboard.

Cut the eyes and mouth from the second picture. Turn them upside down and glue them over the eyes and mouth of the third picture. Glue this picture to a piece of posterboard.

To Do and Notice
(5 minutes or more)

Place both pictures upside down before letting anyone view them. Then have the viewers look at the two upside-down pictures. Finally, have the viewers look at both pictures right-side up.

Your viewers may or may not recognize the personality in your picture when the picture is upside down. The two upside-down views may look strange (one perhaps stranger than the other); but turn them right-side up and one looks normal, while the other may look grotesque.

What's Going On?

Since an upside-down face is not a familiar point of view, your viewers may not have noticed that one of the pictures has been altered. It's only when the photos are turned right-side up, and the view is more familiar, that you notice the real difference.

○ ○ ○ ○ ○ ○ **etc.** ○ ○ ○ ○ ○ ○

Make 35 mm slides of the faces of familiar personalities from magazines and newspapers, as well as live photos of friends. Show the slides upside down and have people try to identify them. Then show the slides right-side up. Interesting!

Whirling Watcher

When you view short bursts of moving images, you see some interesting effects.

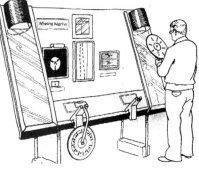

▶ A series of slits moving rapidly past your eye allows you to see images in short bursts. Such rapid but fragmented views of moving objects can make the objects appear to jerk along, change speed, or even move backward.

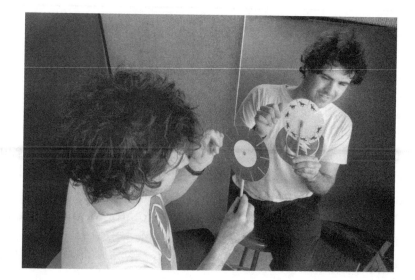

Materials ► Copy of the stroboscope disk template provided.

► Posterboard for backing the stroboscope
disk.

► Access to a copy machine.

► A glue stick or suitable adhesive for mounting the disk to the backing.

► A rotator for the stroboscope disk. You can
use a variable-speed electric drill, hand
drill, portable electric mixer, electric screwdriver, or pencil and pushpin.

► Scissors or utility knife.

► Running (or siphoned) water.

► Black posterboard to use as a background
for the water.

► A large mirror.

► A partner. Adult help.

► Optional: adhesive-backed Velcro™.

Assembly
(30 minutes or less)

Make a copy of the stroboscope pattern on the next page. Enlarge
it if you wish. Cut out the pattern and glue it to the posterboard.

Cut the posterboard to the same shape as the stroboscope, including the slits. You can cut with a good pair of scissors alone,
or use scissors in combination with a utility knife.

Mount the stroboscope disk on the rotator. You can use adhesive Velcro™ to mount the disk to the electric drill or other device. If you use a drill with a chuck, you can use a bolt as a shaft,

with two nuts to hold the disk. (You can also make a simple manual rotator by simply sticking the pushpin through the center of the disk and into the end of a pencil or wooden dowel.)

To Do and Notice
(15 minutes or more)

Close one eye. Hold the stroboscope so that the side with the horses is facing away from you, and so that you can see through a slit with your open eye. Spin the disk and look through the slits at your surroundings. Notice that you can see the entire scene on the other side of the disk, not just one small strip of it.

Try spinning the disk faster, then slower, and compare the results.

Have a friend hold a hand so that you can see it through the spinning disk. Ask your friend to move his or her hand from side to side. Notice that the movement you see is jerky rather than smooth. Have your friend move his or her hand rapidly, and then slowly. Notice that the amount of jerkiness changes as the speed of the hand movement changes.

Stand facing a mirror, and hold the disk and rotator in front of you. Be sure the disk is mounted on the rotator so that the horses are facing the mirror. Spin the disk and watch its reflection in the mirror through one of the slits. Concentrate your attention on one of the horses, and you will see it gallop!

Let water run slowly enough to produce a stream that breaks up into separate droplets as it falls. Place a black background behind the well-illuminated drops of water. Look through the spinning stroboscope and watch the water-droplets fall in slow motion. Vary the stroboscope's speed and see if you can make the water-droplets stand still or even look as if they are moving upward.

What's Going On?

As the strobe disk rotates, a series of open slits moves rapidly past your eye. Each time a slit passes your eye, you see a glimpse of the scene on the far side of the disk. Each open-slit image lingers in your eye and brain long enough to merge with the next image. This phenomenon, called *persistence of vision*, can combine the glimpses in such a way that your brain sees continuous motion.

If an object in the scene moves, your eye and brain can draw incorrect conclusions about that object's motion. When you look at the stream of water, for example, one slit allows you to view a droplet in a particular position. Depending on how fast your strobe is turning, the next slit might let you see a different droplet just slightly below the position of the one previously viewed. Your eye–brain system interprets the combined views as the slow motion of a single droplet. If the second view catches the droplet in a position just above that of the previous view, the droplet will seem to rise.

○ ○ ○ ○ ○ ○   **etc.**   ○ ○ ○ ○ ○ ○

Place a bicycle upside down and spin a wheel. Look at the spinning spokes through the slits in the Whirling Watcher. You can see the spokes stop, or move slowly forward and backward, like the wheels on a moving stagecoach in an old Western. In modern Westerns, special wheels with unevenly spaced spokes are put on the stagecoaches to avoid the strange appearance of backward rotation when the moving wheels are filmed. A regular set of wheels with evenly spaced spokes is used for scenes in which the stagecoach is not moving.

You can exercise your creativity by making your own moving pictures. On the opposite side of the Whirling Watcher disk from the horses, in the space between each pair of slots, draw images, each of which is slightly different from its neighbors. (A running stick figure is an easy set of images to start with.) Look through one of the slots at a mirror, just as you did with the horses, and spin the disk.

For more information about devices like this (called *zoetropes, fantascopes,* or *phenakistoscopes*), see the book *Seeing the Light,* by David Falk, Dieter Brill, and David Stork (Harper & Row, 1986, p. 195).

Index

Page numbers in italics indicate illustrations relevant to the topic.